Gross History

Gross
FACTS About
PIRATES

BY MIRA VONNE

raintree
a Capstone company — publishers for children

Raintree is an imprint of Capstone Global Library Limited, a company incorporated in England and Wales having its registered office at 264 Banbury Road, Oxford, OX2 7DY – Registered company number: 6695582

www.raintree.co.uk
myorders@raintree.co.uk

Edited by Mandy Robbins
Designed by Philippa Jenkins
Picture research by Wanda Winch
Production by Steve Walker
Printed and bound in India

ISBN 978 1 4747 5217 6
21 20 19 18
10 9 8 7 6 5 4 3 2 1

British Library Cataloguing in Publication Data
A full catalogue record for this book is available from the British Library.

Photo Credits
AP Images: Matt Rourke, 15; Bridgeman Images: © Look and Learn/Private Collection/Kenneth John Petts, 9, © Look and Learn/Private Collection/Ron Embleton, 13, 19, 27, © Look and Learn/Private Collection/Severino Baraldi, 25, Archives Charmet/Bibliotheque des Arts Decoratifs, Paris, France/Bernard Finegan Gribble, 7, National Geographic Creative/Robert McGinnis, 23; Lukáš Fibrich, 11; Rick Reeves, cover, 5, 29; Shutterstock: irin-k, fly design, Ivan Pernjakovic, 8, Milan M, color splotch design, monkeystock, grunge drip design, Produck, slime bubbles design, Protasov AN, weevil, schankz, 6, Spectral-Design, 20; SuperStock: SuperStock, 17, 21

CONTENTS

The Golden Age of Pirates

From 1690 to 1725, pirates ruled the seas. Some pirates lost limbs or were killed in battle. Others died from diseases. Lucky pirates lived long enough to spend their stolen treasure. But they still had to deal with the gross details of life on a pirate ship.

Stinky sea life

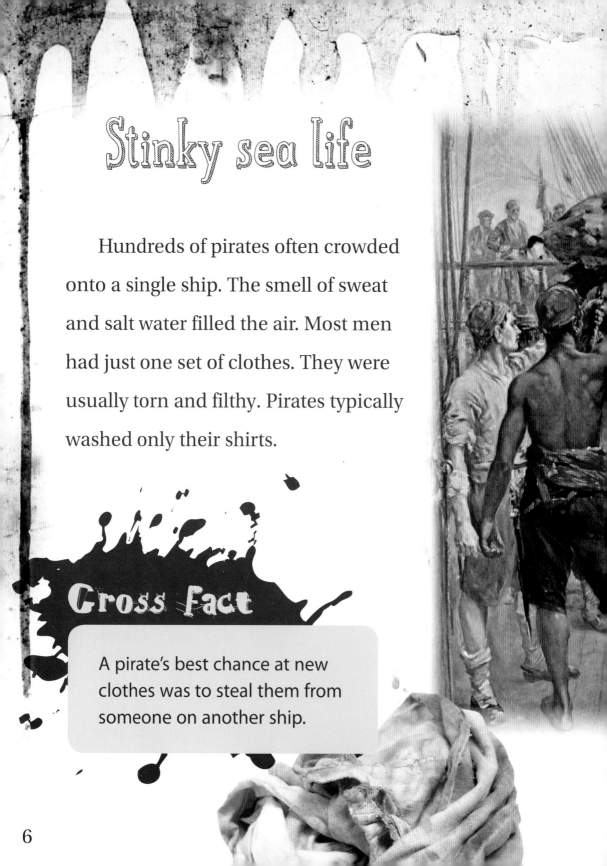

Hundreds of pirates often crowded onto a single ship. The smell of sweat and salt water filled the air. Most men had just one set of clothes. They were usually torn and filthy. Pirates typically washed only their shirts.

Gross Fact

A pirate's best chance at new clothes was to steal them from someone on another ship.

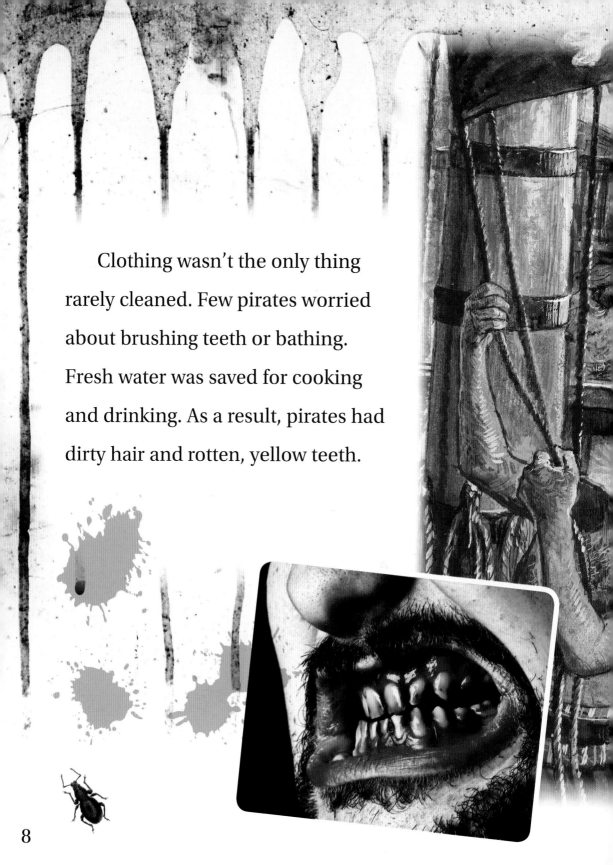

Clothing wasn't the only thing rarely cleaned. Few pirates worried about brushing teeth or bathing. Fresh water was saved for cooking and drinking. As a result, pirates had dirty hair and rotten, yellow teeth.

Most pirates went to the toilet through a hole at one end of the ship. Pirates had to pick the right time for their toilet breaks. During rough waves, the waste sometimes washed back onto the ship.

toilet

Gross grub

Cooks on pirate ships had little training and few supplies. They put salt on vegetables and meat to make it last longer. As time went on, food rotted. Cooks hid the rotten taste with spices.

Gross Fact

Cooks made meals in large kettles over fires. On windy days pirates did not cook. One spark could set the creaky wooden ship on fire.

A pirate's diet often included hardtack. These hard biscuits were made of flour and water. They didn't spoil as fast as meat. Tiny bugs often found their way into hardtack. Hungry pirates ate the biscuits, bugs and all.

Gross Fact

When supplies were low, cooks used fish bones, animal bones and even rats to make a nasty batch of bone soup.

Ready for battle

Pirate battles were disgusting and deadly. Some pirates threw clay pots filled with **sulphur** and rotten fish. Others pushed their way onto enemy ships for hand-to-hand battles. Sharp **cutlasses** caused deep, deadly wounds.

sulphur yellow chemical element used in gunpowder, matches and fertilizer

cutlass short sword with a curved blade

A single pirate ship often carried up to 40 **cannons**. Pirates had to be skilled when firing cannons. A misfire could cause burns or take off an arm. A direct hit could send an enemy ship to the bottom of the sea.

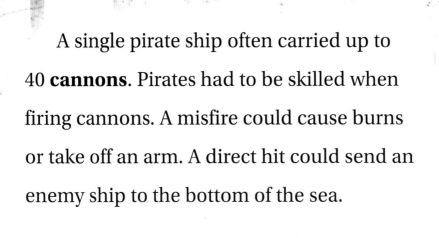

cannon large, heavy gun that usually has wheels and fires explosives

Gross Fact

Blackbeard was one of the most feared pirates of the Golden Age of Pirates. He carried pistols, knives and two swords with him at all times.

Pirates in pain

With little medicine or clean water, battle wounds got **infected**. Arms and legs that didn't heal were removed. Limbs were cut off with a red-hot saw. Pirates hoped the heat would stop the bleeding.

infect cause disease by introducing germs or viruses

Diseases could wipe out entire **crews**. Many pirates suffered from **scurvy**. This painful disease caused loose teeth and rotten gums. If left untreated, victims died.

crew team of people who work together

scurvy deadly disease caused by lack of vitamin C; scurvy produces swollen limbs, bleeding gums and weakness

Gross Fact

To stop scurvy, pirates drank ale with herbs. Later they learned that eating citrus fruit prevented the disease.

Pirate codes

Pirate codes helped captains keep order on their ships. Pirates who broke the rules of the code faced awful punishments. They were often **flogged**. Scars ensured the pirate would never forget this punishment.

flog beat with a whip

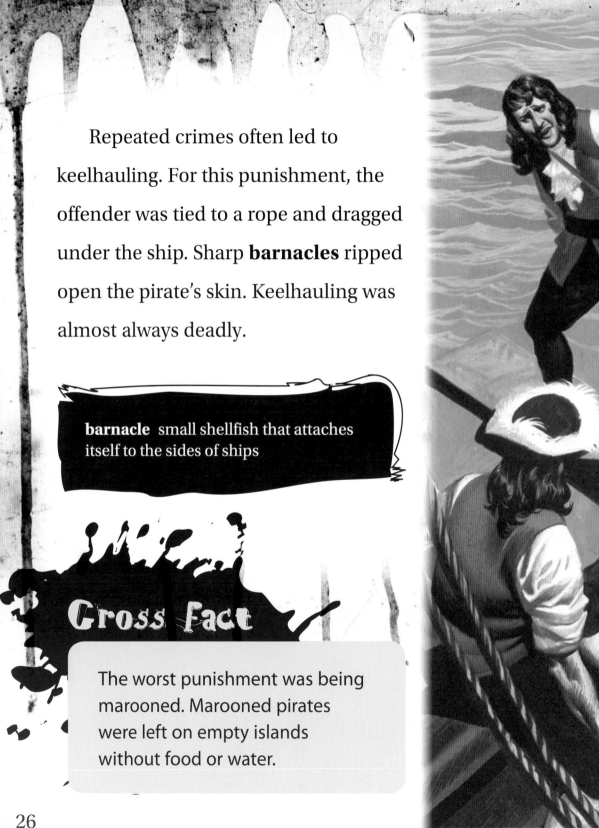

Repeated crimes often led to keelhauling. For this punishment, the offender was tied to a rope and dragged under the ship. Sharp **barnacles** ripped open the pirate's skin. Keelhauling was almost always deadly.

barnacle small shellfish that attaches itself to the sides of ships

Gross Fact

The worst punishment was being marooned. Marooned pirates were left on empty islands without food or water.

End of the Golden Age

Pirates traded life on a disgusting ship for freedom. But their crimes didn't go unnoticed. By the 1720s many pirates were captured and hanged. Their deaths brought an end to the Golden Age of Pirates.

Glossary

barnacle small shellfish that attaches itself to the sides of ships

cannon large, heavy gun that usually has wheels and fires explosives

crew team of people who work together

cutlass short sword with a curved blade

flog beat with a whip

infect cause disease by introducing germs or viruses

maroon leave someone alone on a deserted island

scurvy deadly disease caused by lack of vitamin C; scurvy produces swollen limbs, bleeding gums and weakness

sulphur yellow chemical element used in gunpowder, matches and fertilizer

Read more

An Adventurous History of Pirates (Blast Through the Past),
Izzi Howells (Franklin Watts, 2016)

Pirates (Know It All), Philip Steele (Franklin Watts, 2014)

The Fact or Fiction Behind Pirates (Truth or Busted), Adam
Sutherland (Wayland, 2014)

Websites

www.dkfindout.com/uk/history/pirates/
Find out about pirates, including pirate women, Blackbeard,
the Jolly Roger flag and pirate adventures, on this website.

www.nationalgeographic.com/pirates/adventure.htm
Visit this website for a history of pirates with pictures,
information, maps and a game.

Comprehension questions

- The details in this book are gross. What other words can you use to describe life on a pirate ship?

- How do the images add information about pirates? Describe some of these images.

- Compare living during the Golden Age of Pirates with living today. Would you want to live during the 1600s? Why or why not?

Index